What people are saying about Levar...

"I strongly agree with everything Levar's F.R.E.E.Z.E. and THINK message stands for. I've been using F.R.E.E.Z.E. concept during my whole career in one way or another. Young or old alike, everyone has goals and in order to reach those goals, you must F.R.E.E.Z.E & THINK."

Shawn Marion,
Dallas Mavericks NBA 2011 World Champion

"Levar Fisher engages, enlightens, and empowers his audience to achieve their personal and professional goals. Levar shares his early years through his football career and talks about the lessons he learned along the way -- lessons his audience can benefit from. Levar is a man of integrity, character, and passion. So don't just read this book, use the life-lessons to help you from making the wrong decisions."

Anthony McPherson,
President & Life Skills Consultant, Gideon Group, Inc.

"My experiences with Levar have always been a blessing! His transparency and ability to communicate to audiences of all ages has been remarkable to watch. Levar has a true gift of being able to make you laugh and cry all in the same hour. I have seen him speak to large groups of many types of people and he is always engaging, intimate and sensitive to his listeners. Time and time again, I enjoy the privilege of being in his presence. I would highly endorse Levar's book because he has proven many times that he is "More than a Pro"—he is a hero who knows where he comes from and is not afraid to share it for the sake of helping others."

Sue Crawford,
Fellowship of Christian Athletes

"As one of Levar's teammates, I can say that he always found a way to motivate the man beside him. He is full of energy and enthusiasm. In order to be in the same room with Levar or on the same field, you better have very high goals and expectations—he expects you to chase greatness. Levar is a big-time believer and a great family man. I enjoyed every minute on and off the field with Levar. He was a perfect teammate and still a great motivator."

Clayton White,
Running Backs & Special Teams Coordinator, UCONN

"Levar has a magnetic personality anyway, but you put him in front of an audience, and his charisma is off the charts. He has a natural ability for pulling people into his stories. They can visualize the moments with him—laughing and crying when he talks about his "near misses" as a youth and actually cheering when he talks about his wins as an athlete. I know from my own experience on the speaking circuit that being able to engage people and have them feel your message is the goal. I've never heard a speaker who was so gifted at reaching that goal. Levar is exactly what he says he is...more than a pro."

Mary Kurek,
Author and Speaker

"Levar Fisher, as he often says himself, is no winner. But he's definitely not a loser, either. Instead, like all of us, he is a chooser—and he's choosing success in LIFE! After his NFL career was cut short by injury, Levar could have allowed bitterness or self-pity to defeat him and derail his future. Instead he has chosen to share what he's learned in life with others, motivating them to consider the consequences of their daily choices and to become the person God made them to be. He is a gifted storyteller, whose humor and homespun wit make him a hit with any audience. Best of all, he's genuine—a committed follower of the Lord Jesus Christ and a loving husband and a devoted dad to two daughters. We've enjoyed his speaking ministry at our multi-site church, and I'm proud to call him my friend.

Jerry McQuay,
Senior Pastor, Christian Life Center

"Levar Fisher is a pillar of strength, wisdom and passion all rolled into one. Levar brilliantly delivers a message of hope to audiences everywhere. His commitment to the youth, his ability to speak and captivate their hearts, is truly a God-given gift that is transforming lives. He not only delivers a message of hope, wisdom, and encouragement, he also lives it every day. Levar is not a just another husband, father, and former professional athlete with a *positive* message….he *is* the message, alive and in living color. Take time to glean from someone who has been there, done that, and has the victory t-shirt to show for it. Read *his* story and find hope and encouragement for your tomorrow."

Dorothy Caldwell,
Chaplain, WNBA Chicago Sky

"From my experience working with Levar, he is a man of valor, strength, and integrity. I appreciate his leadership and direct communication but most of all, I have the utmost respect for Levar as a husband and father. When I first read the F.R.E.E.Z.E. THINK ABOUT IT content, I knew it was a winning combination of Levar's wit, wisdom, and passion for changing the lives of young people across the country. Gracious, filled with character, sincere…that's Levar."

Michelle Hill,
President of Winning Proof, Strong Copy Quarterback

"While hosting forums across the country during our tour of One Million Mentors Campaign to Save Our Kids, I have seen first hand that our youth need us more than ever. I commend and support Levar on writing his book because it will change lives. It's true that if we just FREEZE before making decisions, we will have a better outcome."

George Willborn,
Co-Host of the Michael Baisden Show & Comedian

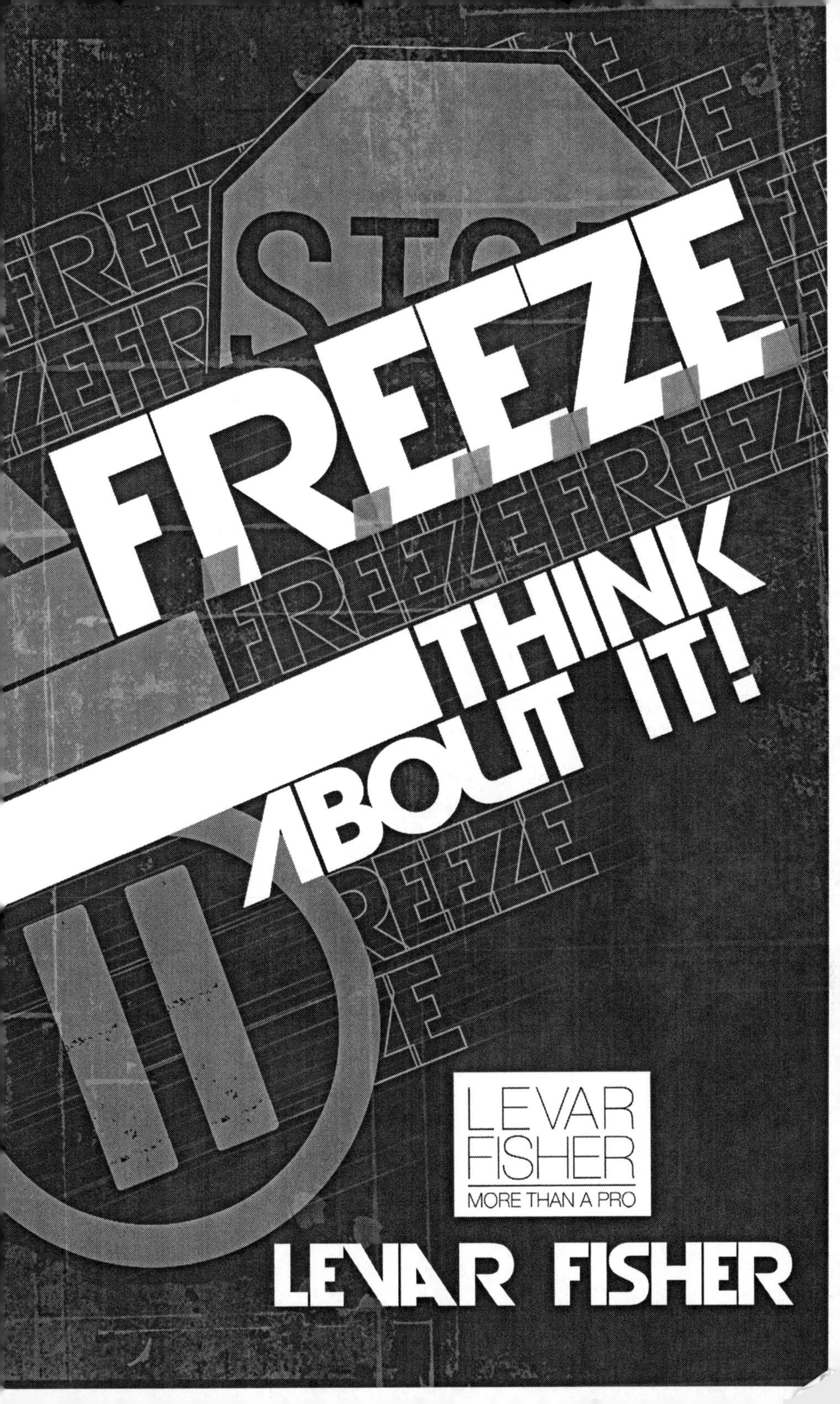

F.R.E.E.Z.E.
Think About It

Published by
Levar Fisher, Inc. | More Than a Pro *Publishing*
4710 Lincoln Highway Suite 268
Matteson, IL 60443
www.levarfisher.com
866-574-4PRO (4776)

Publishers: Levar and Jacinta Fisher
Editorial Director: Yvonne Rose | Quality Press
Production Coordinators: Jacinta Fisher & Yvonne Rose
Interior Design: The Printed Page
Cover Design: Jason X. Hudson | Point 25 Designs
Back Cover Photo: Robert Pears | Robert Pears Photography

ALL RIGHTS RESERVED
No part of this publication may be reproduced or transmitted in any form or by any means, electronic or mechanical, including photocopy, recording, or any information storage and retrieval system now known to be invented, without permission in writing from the publisher, except by reviewer who wishes to quote brief passages in connection with a review written for inclusion in magazine, newspaper or broadcast.

The stories in this book are based on real people and true events. Some names have been changed to protect their identity and privacy.

More Than a Pro Books are available at special discounts for bulk purchases, sales promotions, fund raising or educational purposes by calling 866-574-4PRO (4776) or email: orders@levarfisher.com

Copyright © 2011 Levar Fisher
ISBN # 978-0-9835841-1-7
Library of Congress Control Number: 2011913767

Dedication

"This is for every person who has a dream, but can't imagine it happening because of mistakes or bad situations in your life. I am proof that there is no bully big enough to kick you so far down and no mistake so bad that you can't find a way to grab that dream. Please believe that as long as you have the heart… I've got the help."

To my beautiful mother, Dora Fisher, who's suffering from Alzheimer's; you taught me to always keep my head up no matter what life tends to throw at me. When I got into trouble as a young man, you would always say in a soothing voice while rubbing on my head, "Do better next time."

To my wife, Jacinta Fisher, who has been by my side, literally holding my hand through every phase our life enters. You have continually urged, pushed, and helped me to pass over what my comfort zone would allow. You are truly my rock and better half.

To my two amazing daughters, Isys and Zoey Fisher, I used to think I was a tough guy but not anymore. You two beautiful, young blessings from above have melted my heart; you are my life.

F.R.E.E.Z.E   Think About It

To my family and friends, thank you for all the help and support.

To the youth, your future is as bright as you'll allow it to be. Thank you for inspiring me to write this book.

Acknowledgments

I gratefully acknowledge the contributions of the youth who have touched my life, and allowed me to share their stories and heartfelt testimonies, which made this book and its content possible.

In particular, I am grateful for the time and input of Tony & Yvonne Rose, Mary Kurek, Michelle Hill, Aleena Johnson, Ilona Dolo, Jason Gill, Susan Coleman, Sir Demetrius Everett, Harold & Rachelle Blackmon, and every other person that has given a helping hand.

I am especially thankful for my wife, my publicist, my head of marketing, Jacinta Fisher. You work so hard with one thing in mind, to help people.

F.R.E.E.Z.E   Think About It

Contents

Dedication	vii
Acknowledgments	ix
Foreword	xiii
Introduction	1
My Story—Hold Onto Your Dreams	5
Chapter 1 F.R.E.E.Z.E—Think About It	9
Chapter 2 F = Focus on what's important	11
Chapter 3 R = Realize who YOU are	21
Chapter 4 E = Eliminate Negative Influences	27
Chapter 5 E = Encourage others	39
Chapter 6 Z = Zone in on YOUR goals	47
Chapter 7 E = Expect Success	53
Conclusion—You Do Have A Choice	59
F.R.E.E.Z.E. Photos	61
About The Author	67
Appendix A: These are Your Facts	69
Appendix B: Sources	77
Appendix C: National Help Resources for Teens	79

F.R.E.E.Z.E   Think About It

Foreword

I first met Levar Fisher in December of 2010. The minute I saw him I knew I liked him. There was something honest and genuine about his energy—and he had the greatest smile.

I told him I owned a seminar company and had been teaching principles of success around the world for almost 30 years. I said that I taught a powerful and unique system for setting goals and creating plans and that the basis of my seminar was the irrefutable fact that *anyone* can live their passion no matter how big or outrageous it was—and no matter where they've come from or who has told them they can't.

I shared with him that some of my greatest inspiration came from the 50 American Idols I had interviewed for the book I co-authored, *Chicken Soup for the American Idol Soul.* These were young people who came from poverty and were homeless, who had lost friends to violence, who had incurable diseases, who had battled addiction, and who had seen and lived things in their short lives that many of us couldn't imagine—yet they didn't use any of it as an excuse to abandon their dreams.

Levar and I soon discovered that we spoke the same language and that our teachings paralleled each other's in many ways. We both teach to focus on your goals and don't be dissuaded by the discouragement committee; to know who you are and what you are capable of and don't give up at the first sign of an obstacle (or the second or third); to avoid negative influences, especially those people who somehow see your desire to succeed as a threat and want to hold you back; to support and encourage other people's dreams, which is one of the quickest and surest ways to reach your own; and to live each day with positive expectations of success, since we will always attract to ourselves whatever is our dominant thought.

But Levar has done something with his vast knowledge of how to win the game of life that to me is extraordinary. Instead of taking his natural charisma and renown as a former NFL player and speaking in corporations where he could be paid handsome sums, he's chosen to devote his life to the youth of our nation. The message of his outstanding F.R.E.E.Z.E. program and of this book: "Think about the consequences before making a decision that will change your life forever" will save countless young people from the pain of having to live with choices they will later regret.

I consider it a great honor to call Levar Fisher my friend and by contributing this foreword, to play a small part in the success of this book. I highly recommend that you not only read it and apply what Levar teaches but also share it with as many young people as you possibly can. It might be the gesture that turns their life around—or saves it.

—Debra Poneman
Best-selling author and founder and
President of Yes to Success Seminars, Inc.

Foreword

> *"You're not born a winner—*
> *you're not born a loser.*
> *You're what you make yourself be."*
> -Lou Holtz

F.R.E.E.Z.E Think About It

Introduction

How many times have you said things you wish you could've taken back? What was it like when you first did something that you knew you shouldn't have? When you trusted that guy or girl and they did you wrong?

Life is not as simple or as hard as we try to make it sometimes. Take a look back over your short life and imagine for one minute you could go back in time and change some of the bonehead decisions you've made. Imagine what the outcome would have been if you had that chance over and you could F.R.E.E.Z.E. and think about the consequences. Would you have said those things about your best friend? Would you have broken in and taken those things that didn't belong to you? Would you have had sexual relations with that person?

I'm sure there are so many situations in your past that you are thinking about at this moment. But, can you imagine the different results you would have had?

Life will sometimes place you in hard situations that put you at a crossroads. The decisions you make at these crossroads will determine your future forever. I've bumped my head many times at these crossroads in life. However, if I didn't learn from my mistakes, and grow up through the process, my future would not have been favorable. After finding myself in handcuffs, seeing friends killed, and seeing my sister get pregnant at an early age, F.R.E.E.Z.E. became a part of my life and I didn't even know it.

My goal was to play in the NFL, but my family had always told me that academics were most important in order to achieve great success. I knew I could make it to the NFL, but I had to **Focus on what was important** and avoid the pitfalls I came across. My goals became my focus and failure was not an option. People overlooking me and being bullied at an early age strengthened my focus to not only play in the NFL, but also to be a total success in life personally and professionally.

I **Realized who I was**; what I wanted for my future and who I aspired to be. I learned from the many mistakes I've made in life but really from this one mistake in particular. As a result of that mistake, I was arrested and thrown in the back of a police car; at that moment I made a promise to myself to never let that happen again.

I understood that I had to eliminate the negativity in myself and negative influences around me as well. **Eliminating negative influences** will bring you positive energy, better opportunities to have favorable outcomes in your life. There will be people you may bump into; maybe even your friends or family who don't care about the consequences of their actions. They have given up hope for a better future because they can't see the bigger picture of life. You do not need that negative influence as company; it will only hold you back.

I pride myself on **Encouraging others**. My goal is to provide plenty of positivity and encouragement to the younger generation who lack confidence and don't see a brighter future for themselves. I love to encourage young and old to set goals; short-term and long-term as well as make plans that will allow them to achieve their goals and to understand the importance of good decision-making. I really drive home to our youth the point that the consequences from bad decision-making can destroy the reality of achieving their dreams.

It's very important no matter the age to **Zone in on your Goals**. The awards I was fortunate enough to win at North Carolina State University continued to build confidence in myself that I could make it to the NFL. However, I never got complacent with where I was; I just remained zoned in on my goals. Once, I made it to the NFL, the feeling of the accomplishment overwhelmed me. The saying, "hard work pays off," was right—it truly did. I knew then, like I know now, the decisions I make when coming up against obstacles I face in life will help guide me toward success.

Expecting Success continues to drive me personally and professionally in achieving more goals in life. After being injured and having to retire from the NFL, I know I am still winning. Now, I'm winning through the youth across America- helping them to **Focus, Eliminate negativity, Encourage others, Zone in and Expect** to achieve their goals. You can't truly expect success if you do not **F.R.E.E.Z.E.** and think before making a choice that can negatively change your future.

F.R.E.E.Z.E   Think About It

My Story
Hold On To Your Dreams

"Never let anyone tell you what you cannot do or what you cannot achieve."
—Levar Fisher

Has anyone ever looked at you like you were the biggest loser in the world? Did they look at you as if they thought they were better than you?

My whole life, people looked down on me. Maybe it was because I didn't come from a great neighborhood or because I was a chubby kid. It didn't help either that my four brothers got into lots of trouble when they were younger so people labeled me a troublemaker as well. And speaking of labeling...

I was in the middle of my fifth grade math lesson and I remember this day as if it was yesterday.

"Pick me! Pick me!" I wanted her, at the very least, to look in my direction. But so did everyone else.

The teacher walked in and told us how important it was to do well in school, and explained that she could, with just one glance, look around the room and tell which of us were going to be successful in our lives.

I started stretching my neck and hands, almost standing in my chair at this point. I wanted her to look at me. I wondered if I was going to be successful one day. She slowly walked between each row of desks with a big smile on her face. She made eye contact with everyone she thought was going to be successful—**and** guess what? She never even looked at me.

I felt hurt and discouraged as I looked at her but determined as I thought, *I don't care what you think about me. I AM going to be somebody. I* **WILL** *make my parents proud of me one day, you'll see.*

By the time I was a sophomore in high school, I was the No. 1 linebacker on my team, the No. 1 football player in the county, and among the top linebackers in the state of North Carolina. But I kept working harder.

As a senior in high school, I had several full scholarship offers to play football in college. I could go to pretty much any college I wanted, for free!

I accepted a scholarship offer to North Carolina State University. I remember getting into college and I was still dreaming big and determined more than ever telling everyone, "Oh, I can't wait to go to the NFL."

Even in college, guys mocked me and said, "Yo dude, those NFL guys are big, man! You're not big enough and you're not strong enough!"

Growing up I had learned from my father that I was going to either prove people like that right, or prove them all wrong. So I just smiled at all the haters and thought, **LET THE GAMES BEGIN!**

In my quest for athletic success, I became purpose-driven, living my life "in the zone." I achieved nearly every goal I set out for myself in college. My sophomore year, I made the All- Atlantic Coast Conference (ACC) Football Team which was a great accomplishment for me.

During my junior year, I became an All-American football player. I became the ACC's Defensive Player of the Year and an Academic All-American. I also led the nation in tackles, averaging almost 16 tackles per game. Out of thousands and thousands of college defensive players, I was number one in the country!

My point is—you need to take the negatives that people say to you and about you and make it work in your favor! Use them as your driving force for success.

F.R.E.E.Z.E   Think About It

F.R.E.E.Z.E.
Think About The Consequences
CHAPTER ONE

One day I was sitting with my friend Tucker in the hallway at school when a kid named Roger came running around the corner and "bam"—like a freight train ran right into Tucker. Tucker, after being knocked down, without thinking, jumped up from the ground and 'boom' punched Roger right in the face.

Everything happened so fast, but what happened next changed everything. Roger crumbled to the floor with blood streaming from his nose. His eyes started rolling and flickering very fast. Then all of a sudden, the flickering slowed and stopped. There was no movement at all. Roger was in a coma and weeks later he died.

Just like that, there were two grieving families. Tucker ended up going to jail and he's still there to this day. I can still hear Roger's mom screaming at the funeral, it was truly a tragedy.

Do you see how fast things can happen to change the rest of your life? **Every decision you make TODAY can change your TOMORROW.**

F.R.E.E.Z.E   Think About It

I talk to kids of all ages almost every week so I hear what you're dealing with on a daily basis. Let's face it; some of you are followers like I was in school. Followers are open prey to gangs/bad crowds because gangs count on your need to be accepted. Stand up for yourself—then **F.R.E.E.Z.E.** and think about the consequences of your actions BEFORE you allow anyone to make **your** choices for you.

Let's take a look at the acronym **F.R.E.E.Z.E.** My hope is that when it comes to decision-making, it helps you remember to STOP, PAUSE and THINK about the outcome **BEFORE** you act in a non-favorable way.

F = Focus on what's important

R = Realize who YOU are

E = Eliminate Negative Influences

E = Encourage others

Z = Zone in on YOUR goals

E = Expect Success

I will break each letter down so you can really understand. As you read each story, ask yourself how you would have done things differently based on the F.R.E.E.Z.E. acronym. You will start to understand why **F.R.E.E.Z.E.** is so important for the decisions you're making TODAY and how one bad choice can change your TOMORROW forever.

Focus On What's Important
CHAPTER TWO

What's important to you in life? Is it school, sports, family, or are you the type of person that focuses all his/her energy into fitting in with a certain crowd? I can be honest and tell you that earlier in my life I was a follower. A follower lets other people make their decisions for them. Don't let others negatively influence your thoughts and behavior. Decide and **FOCUS** on what's important to **YOU** and stand your ground in all situations.

You may feel pressured to think that being on the honor roll is not cool; that being smart is for nerds. But, in the end, regardless of who says what about you, academics are the most important. Statistics show that the harder you study, the smarter you'll be and the better your life will turn out.

"There are no secrets to success. It is the result of preparation, hard work, and learning from failure."
—Colin Powell, Four Star General

If you've had someone tell you that you won't amount to anything, those are just words; it doesn't have to shape who you are, or your future. Learn to tune out negativity; aka HATERS.

Learn how to build your own support system and rely on positive people who will help you nurture your dream.

It's important to create your own support team; people who push you toward your goals and see things in you that you don't see in yourself. You may already have these people in your life and not even realize it. It could be a teacher, coach, family member or maybe all.

You can lean on them, ask them for help, and let them lift you up when you're down.

My high school football coach Mickey helped me to stay straight on my path so I could end up with a full-ride scholarship to NC State. He saw greatness within me when all I saw and felt was failure. He focused on my potential and encouraged me to live up to it.

Learn who your support team is and use them, even the so-called HATERS in your life; let all those HATERS become motivators.

There's so much negative peer pressure to try drugs or alcohol of any kind. **F.R.E.E.Z.E.** and decide **this minute** that you're not going to be a follower and let your friends lead you down that self-destructive road.

> *"A man who stands for nothing will fall for anything."*
> —Malcolm X

Focus On What's Important
Youth Story

Jasmine, a beautiful, intelligent 16-year old with the world at her fingertips, clutched her stomach as she screamed in pain. Her face, distorted from trying to endure the overwhelming cramps, she knew the abortion pill was doing its job.

With each gut wrenching cramp, Jasmine thought back to her mom's diligent efforts to teach her to stay sex-free until marriage.

The staying pure speeches had been making an impact until high school when Jasmine started hanging with some promiscuous, aka FAST, rowdy girls at school. Crude jokes, flirting with anyone who would pay attention to them, and bragging about their latest sexual conquests were the norm in this circle. Wanting attention and longing for acceptance, Jasmine bought into the group's lifestyle, a little at first, then went all in. It didn't take long before Jasmine *became* one of those girls.

She kept hanging' with the bad crowd even after she dropped out of high school two weeks before graduating, without her diploma.

Two DUI's within a six-month period and stopped by police while possessing a bag of drugs, handed Jasmine a felony charge and landed her in jail all while she was pregnant.

A steady stream of poor choices created a bad situation that still haunts her several years later. At age 30, Jasmine has not only had four kids by four different dads, she has sold her body numerous times just to make a few bucks. She's contracted an incurable STD and she continues to reap the physical effects from the abortion pills. This is quite a list of negative accomplishments for a young lady that was so beautiful and so full of promise.

Celebrity Story

Plaxico Burress, NFL Wide Receiver

Michigan State University's student-athlete Plaxico Burress had always aspired to become a professional football player. His dream came true when he was picked in the first round of the 2000 NFL Draft.

Officially drafted by the Pittsburgh Steelers, Plaxico's football career began to soar, catching the eyes of the New York Giants. By 2005, he left the Steelers to become a member of the Giants. What used to be his long time desire was suddenly becoming his reality, but little did he know, he would be the reason his highly anticipated dreams would turn into a horrifying ending nightmare.

One night, Plaxico made the decision to carry a gun into a New York City nightclub for protection. While enjoying himself at the party, Plaxico's gun, which was tucked into the waistband of his sweat pants, began sliding down his leg. In an attempt to stop the falling weapon, Plaxico accidentally pulled the trigger. In an instant, his once smart decision was no longer seen as smart. He had mistakenly shot himself in the thigh. In addition to his new self-inflicted injury, Plaxico faced police charges, criminal possession of a handgun, and turned himself in. As a result, he served 2 years in prison.

If Plaxico, in the moment, could have adopted the F.R.E.E.Z.E and think about the consequences concept, his career would not have been put on hold. He did his time and now he is back in the NFL, currently playing with the New York Jets. I hope for his sake he makes better decisions.

Questions

Think About It

If you found yourself in Jasmine's situation, what things would you have done differently?

If Jasmine was your friend, what kind of things would you have said or done to help her?

If you were a star like Plaxico Burress, what things would you do if you felt you needed protection?

If you had a second chance like Plaxico, what kind of life style changes would you make?

F.R.E.E.Z.E Think About It

Form your own opinion and define what's important to YOU.

What is **your** focus? Do you want to save yourself until marriage? Do you want to be an All-American football player? Play in a band? Be a singer? An astronaut? A lawyer? A scientist? A writer? An artist?

"If Your Dream is Big Enough, Facts Really Don't Matter"
—Dexter Yager

What are **your** facts? Maybe you believe you are too skinny or too fat to play a sport well. Maybe the color of your skin makes you think you can't get a certain scholarship. Maybe you believe you're stupid and have been told you won't amount to much. Some people think like I did—that the neighborhood I came from or the mistakes I made in my past would make it impossible for me to reach my dream.

Listen up. I remember sitting in the back of a police car one day after a big mistake with one question on my mind, "How can I still go to college from where I am now?" The **fact** of the matter was—I made a huge mistake that could have cost me my life. But, my dream of playing in the NFL was big enough to turn me around and point me in the right direction. You never know how much you love something until it's taken away. But more about that story later.

Right now, I want to share more facts on how your dreams have to be big enough to carry you through the tough times.

A few years ago, I was badly injured and had to retire from the NFL. There's a **fact**—no more football! I lay in the hospital bed crying like a baby. I needed a new dream and it had to be big enough to pull myself out of my funk of not being able to play football again.

My new venture was enormous. It's about YOU… and every other person who will listen to me or read my material. This dream is bigger than the NFL. I now travel around the globe helping young people learn from my experiences and my mistakes.

I don't want you to think it's easy. It's never easy to think past the facts that could slow you down from fulfilling your goals in your life. But, I'm telling you that you CAN do it. Never let any fact or person get in the way of YOUR big dream.

Be a leader, not a follower. Stay in school, go to college, and "choose" your way out of any kind of deprived situation. I grew up in the country; it wasn't the projects but it was poverty-stricken. For you, it doesn't matter where you live or how you live. Success-minded people rise to the top so rise to the top my friend, go further than even you can imagine.

*"Only as high as I reach can I grow,
only as far as I seek can I go,
only as deep as I look can I see,
only as much as I dream can I be."*
—Karen Ravn

The Facts about Gangs

- Gangs exist in every state, whereas in the 1970s they existed in less than half of the states.

- A gang member is 60 times more likely to experience death by homicide than the general population.

- One-fourth of gang members are aged 15-17.

- The average age for a gang member is 17 to 18 years old.

- There are more males in gangs than females, although the number of females in gangs is on the rise.

F.R.E.E.Z.E Think About It

Realize Who You Are
CHAPTER THREE

Who are YOU? Are you a Star? Are you an Extra? Do you feel like a nobody?

Seriously, ask yourself who you REALLY are and what defines you? If you could look at your inner heart, what would you see? Would you see character and personal morals, or would you see that the lines are blurred? How do you see yourself?

One quick way to find out who you really are is to close your eyes and picture yourself at your own funeral; lay down on your floor and imagine people walking by your casket and whispering things about you to each other, what would they be saying about you?

Once you realize who you are, you have to stand firm in that. You can't be afraid of what others say or think you are. If you're not necessarily confident in yourself, still don't hide. Do your best to figure it out and stay true to yourself.

There will always be people who will attack your identity. The things we go through in life make us who we are or who we become. Don't panic because you may not have it all figured out right now. It doesn't matter what color, gender, mental or physical handicap you may have. You may not even have much money in your family but you CAN still achieve your dreams.

> *"Don't rely on someone else for your happiness and self worth. Only you can be responsible for that. If you can't love and respect yourself—no one else will be able to make that happen. Accept who you are—completely; the good and the bad—and make changes as YOU see fit—not because you think someone else wants you to be different."*
> —Stacey Charter

You can be President, a teacher, a principal, a lawyer, a doctor, a professional athlete, or anything else you can think of. I'm sure you've heard the "You can be whatever you want to be speech" many times. What people fail to say or we fail to hear is that whatever your dream is, it's going to take a lot of hard work and dedication. When most of us hear about the work that needs to happen for our dream to become reality, that's when we get discouraged or we choose to have another dream.

For those of you who are trying to fit in—be the best you, you can be. Build your own personal foundation—a foundation you can stand on for life.

"Your vision of yourself today is just a preview of who you will become."
—Unknown

Knowing who you are will keep you confident and give you a high self-esteem. There's no one that can steal that from you unless you give them permission.

When you decide what's important to you, stick to making that thing happen. Form your own opinions and don't let others distract you from where you want to go in life.

"Never allow someone else's opinion of you to become your reality."
—Les Brown

F.R.E.E.Z.E   Think About It

<u>Realize Who You Are</u>
Youth Story

Take Dwight for instance, his whole life people told him that he was just like his father. He heard it so much he thought he *was* his father. Dwight looked, walked, and talked like his father so much that he forgot who he was inside. His dad was a big man in town—but he was a big man in all the wrong things: drugs, violence, and alcohol.

As Dwight lost himself as he got older, he continued to look to his father for guidance and was actually proud he was entwined in his dad's lifestyle. By the time Dwight was sixteen, bad choices became a part of his life. The first crime would be easy and fast. Dwight would just smack the store clerk over the head and knock him out so he could take the cash, so he thought. But the store clerk didn't go down instantly after the first blow to the head. Dwight continued to hit him over and over; harder and harder he swung until finally, the clerk slumped to the ground.

A first degree murder charge was delivered to Dwight. When Dwight heard the heavy clunk of the prison doors shutting behind him, he knew then that the life he once dreamed of having was completely gone, all because of the decision, the choices, and now the consequences of his actions.

Thirty years later, and some unmentionable situations in prison, Dwight was finally released at age 53. Starting over at 53 with a prison record and no money doesn't sound like a real fun party, does it?

Every man or woman in prison had a dream at some point in their lives. Somehow, they lost their way… made some poor choices… forgot the MAIN thing.

Celebrity Story

Fantasia Barrino, *2004 American Idol Winner*

Fantasia Barrino had physical attributes that were often the focus of negative attention in school. Her peers made fun of her lips, which caused a lack of self-appreciation and personal insecurities.

Fantasia allowed the hurtful words of her peers to become part of her self-image. To make up for the nonexistent relationship she had with herself, she chased after the illusion of relationships and attention of young men.

By the time she was in high school, Fantasia wore tight clothing to gain the attention of her male classmates instead of using her inner beauty and incredible talent of singing. She simply wanted to be noticed. Her world was devastated when she was raped in high school.

Her family was there to reassure her and music consoled her during that difficult time in her life. As a result, she rebuilt her self-esteem and recognized her potential.

At the prompting of her brother, Fantasia decided to audition for a televised singing competition and emerged as the winner of American Idol 2004.

QUESTIONS

<u>Think About It?</u>

Like Dwight, do you look up to someone who may not be the best influence for you?

How would your behavior change, if someone looked up to you?

Do you know someone like Fantasia who has been the brunt of hurtful teasing because of a certain physical attribute?

How would you build that person's self-esteem back up?

If it's been you who has been the brunt of cruel teasing, in what ways can you begin to re-build and believe in yourself so you can do the things you want to accomplish like Fantasia?

Eliminate Negative Influences
CHAPTER FOUR

Identify negative influences that lead to costly mistakes

Remember the story I told you earlier about a big mistake I made? When I was in high school, I sat in a jail cell because of a reckless break-in with my friends.

I pondered the fact that this thoughtless act may be enough to kill my chances of getting into college, much less making it to the NFL.

In fact, one of my friends who was in on the break-in didn't make it out of the house alive. He was shot and killed as he tried to escape.

This experience changed me forever. You can't change your mistakes, but you can learn from them. I became wrapped so tight around my NFL dream that I worked at it non-stop. The saying is right, "You never know how much you love something or someone until it's taken from you."

I thought football was gone forever but thank God, it wasn't. After that episode in my life, I told myself that I would let nothing or no one else pull me from my goal, even if it meant turning away from my buddies. Life is so much longer than high school. You can't let thoughtless mistakes take you down.

> *"The only real mistake is the one from which we learn nothing."*
> —John Powell

Who are you hanging around? Who or what habits get you into trouble? Is it a friend who ditches school? A druggie? The neighborhood you live in? Gang recruiting? Do these things draw you into becoming someone you're not? Think about the music, TV shows, video games, and social media you're spending time on.

Identify the people and places that go against the definition of "who you are" and what you and your family stand for. Do the people you call friends build you up and make you better or bring you down and into trouble? If your friends are not helping you get closer to your dreams but rather further away, they're really not your friends.

> *"No one else can ever make your choices for you. Your choices are yours alone. They are as much a part of you as every breath you will take, every moment of your life."*
> —Dr. Shad Helmstetter's

QUESTIONS

<u>Think About It?</u>

Think of one thing you can do to make sure you're spending time with the right people.

If your friends were trying to talk you into what they call a simple "crime" how would you handle it?

Would you walk away even if your peers are calling you chicken or laughing at you?

Eliminating Negative Influences
Youth Story

When eliminating negative influences from your life it may come down to you just simply "Taking a Stand." My friend Jamal was sitting in his car after football practice waiting on me one day. The nauseating stench of stale beer and smoke permeated the entire inside of his car as I walked up. He was so high that I couldn't believe he was even attempting to drive. He was talking loud and trying to get me to jump in the car to go with him to a party.

I remember saying laughingly, "No way man, are you crazy?" His eyes were blood shot, plus he was slurring his words. I knew who and what was going to be at the party. I also knew that I was working too hard and I needed to stay out of trouble.

But Jamal kept pestering me. "Come on," he said, "Just get in and stop being a punk." After hearing that I almost hopped in.

As I grabbed the car door, in my mind all I could hear was my coach saying to me, "Levar, you gotta keep yourself clean. You've got potential if you don't mess it up."

I knew I had to take a stand. It wasn't about pushing my friend away—it was about standing up for myself. I finally ended everything by telling Jamal that I would hook up with him later. He got really upset and he sped off, cursing me out. That was one of the hardest and smartest decisions I ever made. Believe me; I wanted to go to the party. At some point in your life you have to understand that every choice has an outcome; good or bad.

That night, Jamal's parents got a phone call—a call no parent ever wants to get.

Drunk out of his mind, their son made a decision to drive. On a dark, twisting road, his car slid out of control and hit a tree. He died that night. Their son's life, marred by drugs and alcohol, came to an abrupt stop.

No more family dinners. No more Christmas mornings or thinking about his future. Gone. He may not have even thought about getting behind the wheel as a conscious decision, but that choice cost him his life. What he left behind was a terrible hurt that his family will carry for the rest of their lives.

"The decisions you make dictate your future and whether it's a bad or good decision, it affects everyone around you."
—Levar Fisher

QUESTIONS

Think About It

Have you ever been asked to participate in an activity that you knew was not going to turn out well?

Would you have done anything else to have a greater outcome to Jamal's story?

How will you react next time you're faced with a dangerous or compromising situation?

Taking a Stand

Taking a stand for yourself on drugs and alcohol is gigantic if you want a future with any hope. It can save your life. But, there are other ways to take a stand for yourself that will determine the kind of life you lead.

I'm talking about standing up for yourself when a sexual opportunity slaps you in the face. Do you really want to risk getting STDs (Sexually Transmitted Diseases)? They're not only embarrassing; they're serious illnesses that often require long-term treatment. They can also affect all of your future relationships.

In the U.S., 1 in 4 sexually active teens become infected with an STD every year. Some common STDs are chlamydia, gonorrhea, genital warts (also known as HPV—human papillomavirus), and herpes.

(Facts in Brief: Teen Sex and Pregnancy, The Alan Guttmacher Institute, New York, 1996.)

Eighty-five percent of them don't even know they have it. This is such a bad problem that The National Institute of Health (NIH) and the Center for Disease Control (CDC) are calling it an epidemic.

While we're talking about sexual diseases, I also want to talk to you about a new phenomenon today called "sexting" where young people exchange explicit photos and messages via mobile phone texting.

According to Wikepedia, some teenagers who have texted photographs of themselves, or of their friends or partners, have been charged with distribution of child pornography, while those who

Eliminate Negative Influences

have received the images have been charged with possession of child pornography.

With the reality of sexting messages going viral via Facebook or MySpace, the chances of a rejected boyfriend or girlfriend spreading your naked or half-naked photos to the public is highly likely.

The emotional shame and damage to ones reputation can last a lifetime from one brief moment of sexting. **Remember**—anyone asking you to share an illicit photo is not respecting you. You can still do right by friends and family; but choose for yourself.

Still others choose to smoke and drink. Some choose promiscuity. Others choose theft and violence. You might have the same opportunity but you can make different choices. Your choices bring you to a bright future.

My closest friends would try to talk me out of going to football practice or to the weight room. They remained my friends but I stopped hanging out with them as much so I could work on reaching my goals. I got to where I wanted to go—most of them didn't.

While in New York, a young girl in the 7th grade approached me after one of my speeches. She told me she was touched by what I had to say in my speech as tears rolled down her cheeks and stained her pretty face with dark lines of mascara. She explained her story in a whisper-like, grief-stricken voice—she had just found out two weeks earlier that she was HIV positive.

Can you imagine getting that kind of news? It only takes ONE sexual encounter to contract any STD, including HIV.

It's bad enough to risk your own health, but what if your decision results in a pregnancy? Now, you've got a life-long concern. Nationally, nearly one million young women under age 20 become pregnant each year. That means close to 2800 teens get pregnant each day.

(Facts in Brief: Teen Sex and Pregnancy, The Alan Guttmacher Institute, New York, 1996.)

> **"Teenage girls are too caught up in being with a guy who's the best for everyone else and not the best for themselves."**
> —Unknown

Celebrity Story
Lindsay Lohan, *Actress*

Lindsay Lohan has starred in countless movies, made appearances on several television shows, and even released a couple of music albums, leading some people to believe she had it all. But nothing could have prepared her for the turn her life and career would take. Lindsay often allowed negative influences to pass in and out of her life, which was often reflected throughout her career.

From bad breakups to bad friends, Lindsay has experienced the highs and lows of life. She has experienced the direct impact people have had on the choices she made. She has experienced what will happen if one does not learn to filter out the negatives.

Thoughtless mistakes such as partying all night with her friends when she should have been filming are one of the reasons the once-superstar began losing her accreditation. Even after being hospitalized, and rehabilitation, Lindsay still fell victim to hanging out with people who were bad influences on her life and career. If she had simply eliminated the negative people in her life, her legacy as an entertainer would be unmistakably profound.

Questions

Think About it

While reading this story, where do you think things went wrong for Lindsay?

Do you think it's that hard to be a star?

How easy or hard do you think it would be for you (being in Lindsay's shoes) to get rid of some of your party animal friends?

Encourage Others
CHAPTER FIVE

Try to encourage others by building their self-esteem, acknowledging that their character is "OK", and reminding them of what's important to them (eg: college, freedom, fun)

Part of being a leader is encouraging others to follow their dreams and not worrying about what others say or think of them. Depending on whom it is, there are certain ways to encourage others; some need a pat on the back and others need a kick in the butt.

Stand up to a friend who's going the wrong way. Befriend the kid who has no self-esteem.

I was the kid who went out for football. I was new on the team and the captain came up to me and said, "Hey. What's your name?" He invited me to lunch with the rest of the team. That experience changed my outlook on football. When I saw how that captain carried himself and how he was liked by everyone, I wanted to be like him.

Look for those who may feel invisible. That's an opportunity for you to grow as a person—you may meet your best friend that day. Be willing to interact and encourage others. Stand up for what's right for others.

Encourage Others
Youth Story

The bully I named Mr. Punk can sum up my early high school years. Even though I was a chubby kid, it never kept me from playing sports or dreaming of someday playing in the NFL.

Nothing made me happier than playing football. I'd run off that field feeling like I was unstoppable. I just knew I was going to make it to the NFL and I'd tell people, "I can't wait until I go pro."

But here's the thing… you can't really brag about a dream that big and be a chubby kid without a bully taking notice.

Turns out Mr. Punk was around one day when I was talking about my NFL plans. It's like he was waiting for the right moment to jump in. He waved his bony finger in my face and called me fat, slow, and weak.

"No way you're ever going to make it to the NFL…or even to college," he yelled.

At this point, other guys were starting to circle me and Mr. Punk was cackling with laughter. There were nearly 50 guys around me pointing and poking fun of me.

I decided right then and there that I'd prove Mr. Punk and everyone else wrong. And, let me tell you, nothing is more fun than proving people wrong.

Today, I wish I could personally thank Mr. Punk because he's one reason I made it to the NFL.

When I look back at my early high school days, I wish somebody would have encouraged me through this tough time. I wish someone would have stood up to Mr. Punk on my behalf. A true friend would have said, "Mr. Punk, it's not true what you're saying about Levar." If that had happened, the situation wouldn't have been so tough.

QUESTIONS

<u>Think About It?</u>

Do you have a Mr. Punk in your life?

How do you deal with the verbal lashes bullies or "so-called" friends send your way?

Can you think of three ways to overcome the Mr. Punk's in your life?

Have you been there to support and encourage your friends who have been bullied by a Mr. Punk?

Bullying and Being Bullied

Bullying is a serious issue in schools today. Schools, governments, and organizations are taking steps to create real consequences for bullies. According to the Journal of the American Medical Association, Almost 30 percent of teens in the United States (or over 5.7 million) are estimated to be involved in school bullying as either a bully, a target of teen bullying, or both. In a recent national survey of students in grades 6 to 10, 13 percent reported bullying others, 11 percent reported being the target of school bullies, and another 6 percent said they bullied others and were bullied themselves.

Limited available data suggest that teen bullying is much more common among younger teens than older teens. As teens grow older, they are less likely to bully others and to be the targets of bullies.

Cyber-Bullying

Today, with youths having increased exposure to the internet, cyber-bullying is growing at an alarming rate.

Even though cyber-bullying occurs online, the emotional and physical consequences can be just as damaging. In some cases, cyber-bullying has escalated to face-to-face contact involving threats, humiliation, and sexual intimidation and there have been reports of murder, suicides, and beatings in connection with cyber-bullying.

According to an iSafe survey:

- 58 percent of kids report that someone has been hurtful or mean to them online.
- 21 percent of kids claim that they have received threatening messages, either by email, through social media accounts or text messaging.

- 35 percent of kids say that they have received threats online.
- 53 percent of kids admit that they have said **something mean to someone else online.**

After the Mr. Punk incident, my brothers and friends encouraged me to keep my head up.

Encourage others you know by telling them something good about life. Make it your goal to tell someone one positive thing about themselves at least once a day. You'll notice that kids will want to hang around you more because they're starving for some positive words.

> *"The bullying was hideous and relentless, and we turned it around by making ourselves celebrities."*
> —Julian Clary, *Comedian*

Celebrity Story
T.I., *Rapper & Actor*

Though popular rapper T.I. has had numerous issues with authority, he has never stopped helping the well-being of others, exemplified through his television show, *Road to Redemption, in 2009.* Through the show T.I. planned to change the lives of several teenagers before his jail sentencing.

His goal was to divert them from a life of crime using the mistakes he had once made and the lifelong lessons he had learned. Though his show focused specifically on seven teenagers, his outreach was televised for teenagers all over the world. T.I. was on a mission to uplift anyone who needed a hand. His show was instilled with life lessons like the values of never quitting, focusing on the positives, and not allowing one's environment to become the definition of who they are.

In 2010, T.I. continued to extend his hand to others by talking a man out of committing suicide. Aside from his skyrocketing rap career, T.I.'s selfless actions are also one of the reasons he is publicized for raising the spirit of those around him.

Unfortunately, shortly after T.I.'s release in 2010 after a year in prison, he made another bad decision and landed himself right back into prison. It seems as though T.I. should practice what he preaches but I'm not judging, everyone makes mistakes, F.R.E.E.Z.E. and think about it.

F.R.E.E.Z.E   Think About It

Zone In On Your Goals
CHAPTER SIX

The first thing about goals is that you have to figure out what exactly they are and then create a plan to make them happen. Put that plan up where you can see it every day! Either as you walk out of your room or place it on your mirror—somewhere that it's going to get your attention.

Identify SOMETHING you want to become, SOMETHING you want to accomplish. Write it down and be as specific as possible. Does it have to do with Family? Education? Career? Leadership? Saving the earth?

Have faith that your goals are going to work!

Now, think about how each life situation you're confronted with affects the overall success of your goals. If you make decisions with your end goal in mind, it'll be easier to say yes or no when certain situations come your way.

If your dreams are big enough, the "facts" don't matter. *Negative statistics and media gloom about certain ethnic or socio-economic groups may go against your dreams but* **hard work and determination can go against the "facts."**

Know that it will take hard work to accomplish your goals so be patient. Don't let obstacles get in the way when you're "in the zone."

Shawn Marion
Dallas Mavericks, NBA 2011 World Champion

Shawn Marion knows all too well how to zone in on his goals. Besides being an NBA champion, he started the Shawn Marion Foundation, which helps single parent families. According to Shawn, "I am doing this for single parent families on Christmas Day because I know what it feels like to grow up and have sneakers so old and worn that I had to avoid puddles so that the socks protruding through the soles of my shoes would not get soaked because my mother could not afford new sneakers," said Marion.

"I know what it feels like to have nothing. My mom is a wonderful and strong woman who worked two jobs for a long time to put food on the table to feed us. To come from nothing to something is a blessing and I want to be a blessing to others." Shawn zones in on his goals by giving others a chance to succeed.

Zone In On Your Goals
Youth Story

Robert's parents knew when he was born that he was never going to be like other kids. Developmentally disabled and facial features that weren't quite like everyone else, Robert grew up experiencing the sting of brutal comments and teasing by his classmates and neighborhood kids.

Instead of becoming bitter and angry, Robert channeled his uniqueness into his goal of giving to others. Robert had a special gift of showing kindness to anyone who crossed his path. With his toothy smile and awkward movements, Robert's goal was to compliment at least five people a day. He didn't let other's cruel comments to deter him from reaching his daily goal.

Thousands of people were the recipients of Robert's kindness and when Robert passed away, thousands of people attended his funeral as a testament to the impact one "different" child made on their lives.

"Don't go through life, grow through life."
—Eric Butterworth

Celebrity Story
Chris Brown, Singer & Actor

Chris Brown's serenading voice became an instant hit among the ladies in 2005 when he released his self-titled debut album.

Three albums later, plus television and movie roles, he had gained a worldwide fan base. Chris was in his zone.

However, his career took an unfortunate turn when he was hit with domestic violence charges. As a result of so much negative press, Chris had to rebuild his fan base and also his career.

Experience has taught him that once a good reputation is lost, it is not the easiest thing to rebuild. He now spends his days focusing on his goals.

He is choosing to ignore the negative media coverage and directs his attention to his artistic abilities; singing, dancing and acting. Chris Brown zoned in on his goals of becoming a well-known entertainer. He pushes pessimistic criticism to the side and concentrates on his talents.

QUESTIONS
<u>Think About It?</u>

What goals have been pushed to the side in your life due to unfortunate circumstances?

Write down 5 ways you can nurture and protect your goals and dreams.

Like Shawn Marion, how can you reach out to others less fortunate than you on the way to reaching your own goals?

Like Robert, how can you use your unique gifts to impact the lives of others?

Like Chris Brown, how do you push negative criticism aside so you can concentrate on your talent?

F.R.E.E.Z.E   Think About It

Expect **S**uccess
CHAPTER SEVEN

At all times, you should never believe that there will be any other outcome other than personal success.

Thinking otherwise allows negative influences to make us lose sight of ourselves, our goals, and the things that are important to us.

> *"Tough times don't last but tough people do!"*
> —A.C. Green

You may lose some friends, you may endure some bullies, and you may have to work hard to succeed, but you WILL succeed!

Expect Success

Celebrity Story
Keke Palmer, *Actor & Singer*

At the young age of nine, and determined to find success, Keke Palmer auditioned for a role in a stage production but she was rejected for the part.

In support of her dream, her family packed up and moved to Los Angeles where she would be in an environment to pave her own road to stardom.

In spite of audition rejections, she persevered for what she truly wanted. Confident in her own ability to sing and act, Keke knew she was destined to be a star.

She not only landed a starring role in the movie *Akeelah and the Bee*, but her debut song was also used on the soundtrack. She later went on to sign a contract with Disney and made appearances in several other movies and music videos.

Her ambitions were her motivation to make her dreams come true. She expected success and would settle for nothing less. She has won almost half of the twenty awards she has been nominated for.

Keke is also the proud owner of a line of clothing inspired by her Nickelodeon television show, *True Jackson, VP.* With so much of her life ahead of her, Keke Palmer continues to expect nothing but success for herself.

YOU are the star of your own movie! The star ALWAYS succeeds. Don't be an "extra." Extras are always forgotten and never succeed like the stars.

Just like Chris Brown and Keke, things are not always going to go according to your plan—so plan to be successful anyway.

If you expect to be a Pro ball player and you get hurt, then expect to be successful as a team manager, General Manager, or even Owner.

If you expect to be a singer or actor and you haven't received your big break yet, keep persevering, keep knocking on doors.

If you expect to be a teacher or coach, and you're struggling in school, find someone to help you study; put all your energy into your schoolwork.

Put all of your effort into your work, give it everything you have and you WILL be successful.

> *"Don't be afraid to shift your dream because you never know where it'll lead!"*
> —Unknown

No matter what, continue to move forward. Odds may seem like they're stacked against you but continue to progress.

> *"Keep your dreams alive. Understand to achieve anything requires faith and belief in yourself, vision, hard work, determination, and dedication. Remember all things are possible for those who believe."*
> —Yolanda Gail Devers

F.R.E.E.Z.E Think About It

Celebrity Story
Kurt Warner, *NFL Quarterback*

Kurt Warner was a stock clerk at a Hy-Vee grocery store in Cedar Falls making $5.50 an hour in 1994.

Kurt was hoping for a chance in the NFL when Steve Mariucci, coach of the San Francisco 49ers at the time, told Warner he had great potential to be an NFL quarterback but was not quite ready yet.

In 1995, Kurt tried Arena football and signed with the Iowa Barnstormers.

Before the 1998 NFL season, Kurt signed with the Rams as their second string QB. Finally, when he got his chance as a starter, Warner threw three touchdown passes in each of his first three NFL starts. He is the only NFL quarterback in history to accomplish that.

By 1999, he was an NFL Super Bowl champion, becoming the seventh player to win both the league MVP and Super Bowl MVP awards in the same year.

> *"Never underestimate the power of dreams and the influence of the human spirit. We are all the same in this notion. The potential for greatness lives within each of us."*
> —Wilma Rudolph

Expect Success

Attitude defines you just as it did for Kurt. **No one else defines your success.**

But, success is so much more than money or fame. To be truly successful is to want to give back to the environment around you and to the next generation but never forgetting the people who helped you get where you are.

It's living a life of fulfillment and having a positive influence. It's having strong values, character, and living an adventurous life. A successful person possesses a ton of personal power regardless of what others around them are saying and doing.

"Nothing can stop the man with the right mental attitude from achieving his goal; nothing on Earth can help the man with the wrong mental attitude."
—President Thomas Jefferson

F.R.E.E.Z.E   Think About It

Conclusion
You DO Have a Choice

I've warned you about the consequences of bad decision-making, including drugs, alcohol, and sex, etc. but what do you do when you are faced with these decisions? When you're in the moment and one of your friends asks you to get in the car, even though you know he's been drinking, how will you respond? I've been where you are and I know the pressure. But that kind of pressure is no match to what you'll feel like if you make the wrong choice.

Please realize that for every decision you make, there will be a consequence.

Reacting or responding to a situation really fast without thinking steals the time you need to make the correct decision. So, **F.R.E.E.Z.E.** and give yourself a few minutes to consider the consequences first. Don't let others rush you into making snap decisions. This is **YOUR** life…not theirs.

"F.R.E.E.Z.E. can save your life;
it can alter your future but when no one
is around it's you who has to F.R.E.E.Z.E.
—Levar Fisher

F.R.E.E.Z.E   Think About It

F.R.E.E.Z.E. Photos

Levar Fisher #44 NCSU WolfPack Magazine Cover

F.R.E.E.Z.E Think About It

ACC Award Ceremony (left to right) NCSU Players: **Koren Robinson**-*Seattle Seahawks,* **Philip Rivers**-*San Diego Chargers,* **Coach Chuck Amato** *and* **Levar Fisher**-*Arizona Cardinals*

Levar Fisher....More than a Pro

F.R.E.E.Z.E Think About It

Elementary School Assembly

High School Assembly

Youth Conference

F.R.E.E.Z.E   Think About It

Remembering the Game

About the Author

Levar Fisher is an awarded college athlete who became a successful pro, captaining not one—but two NFL teams, and later taking that leadership role to the stage as a sought-after motivational speaker. Surprisingly, Levar's rise to the top isn't because he hasn't made mistakes…*but because he **has** made them…and has learned how to use them.*

Growing up in a small town called Beaufort, North Carolina. Levar didn't find a lot to keep him out of trouble or away from a BK Whopper. Subsequently, he received his first motivation for success from bullies who made fun of his weight and his dreams of playing professional football.

A few years and a lot of hard work later, Levar was recruited by North Carolina State University, attending on a full football scholarship. He made 1st team All-ACC selection in 1999, claiming that honor again in 2000 and 2001, as well as ACC's Defensive Player of the year. He was a Butkus Semi Finalist for Best Linebacker in the Country 2000 and 2001, and a 2000 Bronko Nagurski Finalist (Best Defensive Player in the Country). You don't become that good as a linebacker without a few tackles (try 492 for a career), and when you are really competitive, you lead the nation in tackles per game with (15.1, 166 for the year).

67

F.R.E.E.Z.E   Think About It

In 2002, the star Wolfpacker was drafted by the Arizona Cardinals—17th slot of the second round. New career meant **bigger choices, bigger decisions, bigger consequences**—a completely new life with temptations and lessons that would be hard learned. Levar managed his "lessons" well and built a solid reputation as a leader.

After joining the New Orleans Saints in 2006, an event occurred that every professional athlete fears, a knee injury that would ultimately cause the end of Levar's career. The recovery was long and painful, but reinvention was just one more step in this pro's journey.

Currently, Levar travels around the country speaking and mentoring young and old alike, in an effort to inspire and bring hope. He has been involved in a wide variety of charitable organizations, including the Boys & Girls Clubs, Kids Are Heroes, Fellowship of Christian Athletes, Sports World, Champions for Today, Athletes Against Drugs and Ray of Hope on Earth.

He and his wife, Jacinta are parents of two beautiful girls Isys and Zoey. They live in the Chicago area, where they have established the headquarters for their own speaking and event firm.

Appendix A: These Are Your Facts

YOUR GOALS

Have you ever tried to reach your goals? If not, now is the time.

On a separate sheet of paper write your goals down.

Start with short term goals on one sheet paper and long term on the other. Remember, be as specific as possible when it comes to your goals. If you want to make the team, say what team you want to make. If you would like to lose weight, say how much weight you would like to lose, you get my point. After you finish with your short term goals, hang that sheet of paper up where you can see it several times a day. I hung my goal sheet on my bedroom mirror so I could see it every time I walked into my room.

If you do your part, meaning, studying, working out, practicing and making good choices, please trust me when I say everything else will handle itself.

Before you know it, you will achieve your short term goals and as a result, be closer to your long term goals.

GOOD LUCK AND MUCH SUCCESS.

What are your:

PERSONAL GOALS

SCHOOL GOALS

FAMILY GOALS

CAREER GOAL

Appendix A: These Are Your Facts

YOUR STORY

I would like to hear your story.

Send email to:

mystory@freezeandthink.com

OR

Send mail to:

(Write "My Story" on outside of envelope)

Levar Fisher, Inc. | More Than A Pro
4710 Lincoln Highway, Suite 268
Matteson, IL 60443

PLEDGE II F.R.E.E.Z.E

Visit

www.freezeandthink.com

to join others taking the pledge to F.R.E.E.Z.E. and think about the consequences before making decisions that can change your life forever.

Appendix A: These Are Your Facts

Hold On To Your Dreams

It seemed like everyone had looked down on him as though they or their kids were better than he was. They assumed that he was not going to make it. They assumed that he could not succeed. Growing up like that could do two things to a child. It could have steered him away from his dreams and goals, or pushed him closer. In his specific case, it was closer. He found out at an early age that, if his dreams were big enough, the facts of his life did not matter. This is the true story of Levar Fisher, the personal experiences of being bullied as a child, and the bad decisions that could have changed his life. He openly shares how he learned from his mistakes, and how he used being bullied as his motivation. In this humorous but heartfelt read, Levar encourages the youth to hold on to their dreams and challenges them to never let go!

"Dreams do come true but IT STARTS WITH A DREAM!"

ISBN: 978-0-9835841-0-0 • Softcover • 48 pages • $9.99

Available in eBook

ORDER TODAY!
Some additional products and resources from our online store.

Visit www.freezeandthink.com/shop

Books — $9.99 - $14.99
For youth, educators and parents

eBooks — $6.99 - $10.99
Now available for both Books

Bookmarks — $.99
Display Levar's F.R.E.E.Z.E message

Banners — $99.00
Display Levar's mantra in hallways

Posters — $4.99
Perfect for the classroom and students

T-Shirts — $9.99 - $12.99
Wearable Reminder - in 2 styles

Wristbands — $2.49
"F.R.E.E.Z.E. & THINK"
"FREEZE THINK ABOUT IT"

1" inch Wristbands — $4.99
Available in Black Only with F.R.E.E.Z.E.

Drawstring Backpack — $9.99
Available in Red & Black Only with F.R.E.E.Z.E. Logo

Landyard — $2.99
F.R.E.E.Z.E Logo

HOW TO CONTACT
LEVAR FISHER

CALL US OR VISIT OUR WEBSITE TODAY

To find out how to book Levar Fisher

for your next event

Phone

866.574.4PRO (4776)

Websites

www.levarfisher.com

www.freezeandthink.com

Email

levar@levarfisher.com

Mailing Address

Levar Fisher, Inc. | More Than A Pro

4710 Lincoln Highway, Suite 268

Matteson, IL 60443

Follow Levar Fisher

www.Facebook.com/levarfisher

www.Twitter.com/levarfisher

Appendix B: Sources

http://www.soundvision.com/Info/teens/stat.asp

http://www.americanathleticinstitute.org/response-ability/?p=361

http://www.troubledteen101.com/articles19.html

http://www.essortment.com/articles/hotline_100016.htm

http://en.wikipedia.org/wiki/Gail_Devers

http://en.wikipedia.org/wiki/Wilma_Rudolph

http://en.wikipedia.org/wiki/Kurt_Warner

F.R.E.E.Z.E Think About It

Appendix C: Resources

NATIONAL HELP RESOURCES FOR TEENS

Adolescent Crisis Intervention & Counseling Nineline
1-800-999-9999

Adoptions- Rosie Adoptions-(if you are pregnant)
1-800-841-0804

AIDS Treatment Information Services
1-800-HIV-0440 (1-800-448-0440)

Al-Anon/Alateen Hotline
Hope and help for young people who are the relatives and friends of a problem drinker.
1-800-344-2666

Alcohol/Drug Abuse Hotline
1-800-662-HELP

Boys Town National Hotline
800-448-3000 24-hour National Hotline
800-842-1488 Business Line
Email: hotline@boystown.org
Website: www.boystown.org

The Boys Town National Hotline is a 24-hour short-term crisis hotline providing callers with crisis counseling, resource information and referrals to local services, with a focus on issues affecting children, families and teens. The hotline is Nationwide—serves the United States, Canada, Puerto Rico, The Virgin Islands, and Guam.

Break the Cycle
1-888-988-TEEN for teens who have questions about domestic and dating violence.

Bullying Websites:

safeyouth.org
keepkidshealthy.com

stopbullyingnow.com
teen-matters.com
kidshealth.org
familyfirstaid.org/bullying.html

CHADD-Children & Adults with Attention Deficit/ Hyperactivity Disorder
1-800-233-4050

Child-Help USA
1-800-422-4453 (24-hour toll free)
Assists Teens with any problem and is also available from Mexico and Canada

Cocaine Help Line
1-800-COCAINE (1-800-262-2463)

24-Hour Cocaine Hotline
1-800-992-9239

Domestic Violence Hotline/Child Abuse
800-4-A-CHILD (800 422 4453)

Appendix C: Resources

Ecstasy Addiction
1-800-468-6933

Food Addiction
1-800-841-1515

Gay, Lesbian, Bisexual, and Transgender (GLBT) Youth Support Line
800-850-8078

Gay & Transgender Hate Crime Hotline
1-800-616-HATE

Herpes Resource Center
1-800-230-6039

Learning Disabilities—(National Center)
1-888-575-7373

Marijuana Anonymous
1-800-766-6779

Mental Health InfoSource
1-800-447-4474

National Adoption Center
1-877-648-4400

National Suicide Prevention Lifeline
1-800-273-TALK (1-888-628-9454 for Spanish-speaking callers) The only federally funded hotline for suicide prevention and intervention. People who are in emotional distress or suicidal crisis can call the Lifeline at any time, from anywhere in the Nation, to talk in English or Spanish with a trained crisis worker who will listen to and assist callers in getting the help they need.

F.R.E.E.Z.E   Think About It

National Runaway Switchboard and Suicide Hotline
1-800-621-4000

National STD Hotline
1-800-227-8922

National Teen Dating Abuse Help
1-866-331-9474

Pet Loss Support Hotline—Grief Counseling Hotline
Iowa State Univ. College of Veterinary Medicine

1-888-ISU-PLSH (1-888-478-7574)

Post-Abortion Project Rachel
1-800-5WE-CARE

(800)222-4764; womenshealth.com

Pregnant Teens
1-800-843-5437 for teens who fear they may be pregnant and teen parents

Tobacco Free Quitline
1-877-724-1090